To My Loving Daughter
Deborah Dianne Fesperman
Who Always Makes Her Father Proud

Other Books in this series of
TRUE ADVENTURE STORIES FROM THE CIVIL WAR:

- **Corydon — The Forgotten Battle Of The Civil War**
  By W. Fred Conway
- **The Most Incredible Prison Escape Of The Civil War**
  By W. Fred Conway
- **The Ruthless Exploits Of Admiral John Winslow —
  Naval Hero Of The Civil War**
  By Paul Ditzel

If not available at your favorite bookstore, you may order direct from the publisher at $9.95 each plus $3.00 shipping and handling.

FBH Publishers
P.O. Box 711, New Albany, IN 47151
Phone 1-800-457-2400

Library of Congress Cataloging in Publication Data
Ditzel, Paul

Quantrill — The Civil War's Wildest Killer
And Other True Adventure Stories
Library of Congress Catalog Number: 91-070890
ISBN 0-925165-06-9

FBH Publishers, P.O. Box 711, New Albany, IN 47151-0711
© Paul Ditzel 1991

Typography and Layout: Pam Jones
Cover: Ron Grunder

QUANTRILL —
THE CIVIL WAR'S
WILDEST KILLER

AND OTHER
TRUE ADVENTURE STORIES
OF THE CIVIL WAR

Paul Ditzel

CONTENTS

Armed with his own personal "death list," the Confederate sadist and plunderer, William Clarke Quantrill, rode against the North, leaving in his wake the bodies of Union soldiers, whether or not they had raised a white flag of surrender.

Quantrill —
The Civil War's
Wildest Killer

Like a long black snake the column of guerrillas wound up the back trails creasing the rolling Kansas hills. On reaching the summit their leader signaled a halt.

"There's Lawrence," William Clarke Quantrill nodded toward the heavy smudge of darkness nestling peacefully in the valley below. "By noon the people down there will be groveling in their own guts."

The lean and grizzled guerrilla chieftain, who wore a makeshift Confederate Cavalry uniform because of the false face of prestige it afforded him, took a deep breath and ran his finger across his forehead, wiping at the sweat and grime of the two-day ride from his Missouri hideout. Quantrill pensively explored his bristling stubble. Four Colt Navy .44's were strapped to his thighs. Extra holsters tied to his saddle bow bulged with more arms.

"Gregg!" snapped Quantrill. "Take five men. Ride down there and look around. We've come this far without a fight and I ain't hankerin' to walk into no ambushes now. But hurry! It'll be daylight before I get a chance to kill me a Yankee!"

Quantrill fidgeted restlessly in the saddle of his sleek brown gelding while waiting for the scouts to return. Most of his 450 raiders dismounted and sprawled alongside the trail. Others were so exhausted they had tied themselves to their saddles to keep from falling off. Now they slouched like

7

drugged men. Those closest to Quantrill noted the look of lust on their leader's leathery face. His eyes gleamed peculiarly and although Quantrill remained silent he never once turned his gaze from the squarish outlines of the city he was about to butcher.

Suddenly he sat up straight.

"To hell with Gregg! He's taking too long. We'll attack now." Turning to his raiders, Quantrill gave them their final orders. "You know what I want, men. Just do like we've rehearsed. Your officers have copies of my death list," Quantrill said, waving a greasy sheet of paper for emphasis. "I want every last man jack of them killed. After they're dead you can help yourselves to anything you want. Then burn everything, houses, stores, even people if they're too scared to come out. But remember — if I catch any of you forcing yourselves on the women instead of killing the men I'll personally shoot you, I don't give a damn who you are, officers or what. Now are there any questions?"

If Quantrill heard the snickers of several bearded renegades he did not acknowledge them. They knew Quantrill meant what he said but if rape was punishable by death at their leader's hands then there were other ways to have some fun at the expense of the helpless young girls and wives. After all, Quantrill could not look everywhere at once.

"If there are no questions, form columns of four."

The men mounted and goaded their horses into attack formation.

"Let's go!" Quantrill shouted.

Like an avalanche the guerrillas spilled down the slopes toward the sleeping city. Comanche war whoops echoed across the valley and the raiders' long unkempt hair streamed out behind the brims of their broad hats. Brilliant red flannel jackets worn by some of them contrasted sharply with those of more severe homespun butternut. Each raider carried at least two Colts. Most carried four. Some six.

The roll call of these Missouri monsters swooping down upon Lawrence read like a Who's Who of Western Badmen: Bill Anderson: on his headstall flapped the scalps of two women. Frank James: he had just about persuaded his brother, Jesse, to begin his apprenticeship in crime under Quantrill. Larkin Scaggs: a defrocked Baptist minister, he was notorious for his ruthlessness and sadism. George Todd. John Jarrett. Cole Younger.

Reaching the plain, Quantrill waved one group of his raiders to branch out and surround Lawrence.

"Don't let anybody escape. If any try, kill 'em!" Quantrill called after them, then motioned for other raiders to gallop up nearby Mount Oread to watch for counterattackers. Quantrill expected only token opposition but he knew federal cavalry from the Olathe garrison would race toward Lawrence the moment they saw the mountain of smoke that soon would billow from the bleeding city. Quantrill therefore had hammered home the importance of making every move, every bullet count.

"The rest of you follow me," Quantrill ordered. "Hit the tent camp first."

With Quantrill leading them the guerrillas thundered down upon the flimsy camp containing recruits for the Fourteenth Kansas and Second Colored Regiments. The Civil War was in its last months and so the recruits were mainly teenagers barely old enough to wear the Union blue. Nobody had bothered to show them how to post a guard. None of them had been issued rifles and most were mercifully asleep when the onslaught struck.

Quantrill gripped his bridle reins tightly in his teeth so

as to keep both hands free to squeeze blazing death into the helpless youngsters. Their startled cries were choked off sharply by the harsh crack of gunfire.

Few recruits got further than the flaps of their tents before they were bowled over by the steamroller surge of the raiders. Those missed by the volley of bullets died brutally under the churning hoofs of the guerrillas' precisely trained mounts. Within minutes, nineteen recruits lay mangled in death, their corpses mashed into the dirt now muddy from their blood.

His appetite whetted by this first taste of spilled blood, Quantrill urged his raiders up Massachusetts Street, the city's main thoroughfare. Quantrill and his men fired wildly right and left at startled citizens who in their sleepiness blundered outside their homes to see what the commotion was about. Most of them fell at their doorsteps before they realized Lawrence was under attack.

Reaching the Eldridge House, a four-story brick hotel which Quantrill figured would be a natural fort, he ordered his men to surround the place and prepare for opposition. But the suddenness of the attack had stupefied Provost Marshal Alex Banks who lived in the Eldridge. A white bedsheet fluttered from his window.

"We'll surrender if you promise you won't do us any harm," Banks shouted down to Quantrill.

"Agreed!" snapped Quantrill, jubilant at this additional stroke of luck that exceeded even his good fortune in reaching Lawrence without opposition from federal patrols honeycombing the hills. Rising up in his saddle he turned to his men. "The city's ours! She's ours, do you hear? Spare the hotel but nothing else! Kill everyone who resists!" he flayed his arms. "And then burn the place out!"

Quantrill's frenzied joy sparked the powderkeg fury bottled up inside the renegades and for the next four hours he could not have controlled them if he tried. First they broke down the doors of saloons and greedily guzzled whiskey, washing down the dust of their grueling ride and also setting the tempo for the bestial job of death and pillage that Quantrill had coached them to do.

Quantrill chose the Eldridge as his personal plum although he allowed several close friends to share the loot with him, a gesture less magnanimous than it might seem in light of the fact there was ten times more loot in the hotel than he could ever carry alone.

Quantrill systematically robbed men and women, all the while snorting his contempt when wives tearfully begged to keep their wedding rings.

The citizens of Lawrence, struck dumb with terror, sought to flee from the rampaging torrent of raiders. Not a few of these people wondered in baffled horror — before they fell dead with bullets in their backs — how this nightmare could have befallen Lawrence. It just wasn't possible such a massacre could happen, not with all the warnings the city had received. The most recent reached Lawrence only two weeks before the attack. Four hundred volunteers left the wheat fields in the midst of harvesting, and rallied to the alarm which proved false.

Two days before the attack Captain J. A. Pike, commanding two volunteer cavalry units, Company K, Ninth Kansas, and Company D, 11th Kansas, spotted Quantrill's band when it crossed the state line near Aubry.

Not only did Pike decide not to engage the guerrillas, but he neglected to alert commanders of Union garrisons who could have sent troops to aid Pike in any encounter. Perhaps Pike underestimated Quantrill, the human mon-

"I want every last one of them killed. . . .
Take what you want—then burn everything!"

Thomas Nast woodcut Harper's Weekly, 1862

ster whose entire life offered many clues helping to explain the Lawrence massacre.

Born July 31st, 1837, in Hagerstown, Maryland, the eldest of eight children, Quantrill preferred to be alone in his youth. Shunned by his playmates because of his streak of cruelty, Quantrill caught snakes in the woods near his home and for kicks nailed them to trees and watched their dying contortions. Similarly he trapped stray dogs and cats and slowly wrung their necks.

Leaving home in his teens, Quantrill headed west and hired out as a school teacher in Mendota, Illinois, a job which startled everyone back home. But this career did not last long. Quantrill murdered a man during a fight in a lumber yard and escaped prosecution by claiming self-defense.

A killer at eighteen, Quantrill continued west, reaching Lawrence in 1858 where he threw in his lot with a gang of Kansas River wharf rats who schooled him in petty crime. Eventually, however, Quantrill pushed his luck too far and the Lawrence sheriff went after him on a horse theft charge, but Quantrill sneaked out of the city before the law caught up with him.

Quantrill's warped sense of right and wrong interpreted the banishment from Lawrence as a personal outrage, and from this seed grew his compulsion to wreak eventual vengeance. Lawrence was the symbol to Quantrill of his crossing the bar into a full time career of crime and he blamed the city for the federal government's subsequent action in formally declaring him an outlaw in March, 1862.

Quantrill organized a band of ruffians into a well-trained guerrilla unit of draft-dodging renegades who smeared a trail of robbery across Kansas under the guise of righting wrongs against the South. He took it upon himself to become an independent fighter for the Confederacy, but let it be known he'd gladly work the other side of the street if the price was right. Quantrill hungered for an official badge of authority and weaseled himself a captain's commission from President Jefferson Davis, a blunder the head of the secessionist states lived to regret.

Armed with an official Confederate commission, Quantrill saw his chance to retaliate against Lawrence, and grabbed it. The city was a stronghold of abolitionist sentiment and Quantrill reasoned he could justify anything under the guise of its being a legitimate target of war. The fact that the city had no fortifications and was of little strategic importance never entered Quantrill's mind.

Quantrill and his band set out on the mission that was to foully brand all of them on the pages of history on August 19th, 1863, and reached Lawrence two days later. After the speedy surrender and plunder of the Eldridge Hotel, Quantrill helped himself to a team of white horses and a buggy and galloped around Lawrence to encourage his men to greater depredations and at the same time derive his own peculiar type of satisfaction from the blood bath.

"You'll have to work fast, boys," he shouted. "Yankee cavalry is bound to be on the way here shortly."

Quantrill cheered his men when they smashed into a clothing store and surprised two youths cowering inside. They forced the boys to fit them with new suits and just as they were leaving Quantrill shot them. The corpses were left to the mercy of the flames chewing into the ransacked store from blazing buildings next door.

Scaggs spotted John Speer, Jr., teenaged son of the editor of the *Lawrence Tribune*, as he fled from the print shop. Scaggs caught up with Speer, robbed the youth, then shot him. Speer fell, severely wounded, a few feet from a blazing residence where he implored other guerrillas to drag him from the unbearable heat.

"Don't worry, Yankee," whooped Quantrill galloping up to Speer. "I'll see you don't burn." The guerrilla blew out the youth's brains with a point-blank shot.

A few blocks away Quantrill paused to gloat while his raiders bulled their way into the home where Judge Louis Carpenter lived with his young bride and his sister. The guerrillas snapped off shots from their hips and dragged the badly wounded judge out into his front yard. When Mrs. Carpenter and the judge's sister saw what the guerrillas intended to do next they threw themselves across his blood-drenched body.

"No!" they shrieked. "Please don't …"

Quantrill barked an obscenity as he threw Carpenter's sister down onto the grass. He yanked the judge's bride up by her braids and held her head so she'd have to watch while he delivered the coup de grace. Mrs. Carpenter screamed, "Oh, God!" and fainted as the shot splashed blood on her face, arms and nightgown.

Further across town Quantrill arrived just in time to see his raiders shoot Edward Fitch, Lawrence's first school teacher, as he tried to shield his wife and three small children in the doorway of his home. A guerrilla put the torch to the house and hustled the dazed Mrs. Fitch and her wailing children from the house, kicking her when she tried to stop long enough to carry out a portrait of her husband. She and her children were flung down in the front yard and forced to watch while the flames consumed the house.

"I beg of you," she implored, "save my husband's body so I can give him a Christian burial. Certainly that's not too much to ask." The liquor crazed guerrillas ignored her tearful pleadings, and Quantrill smiled with satisfaction.

16

The only answer he gave her was to dash through the heat to yank off the dead man's boots which he claimed as his personal souvenir.

An enormous cloud of black smoke was mushrooming high over the Lawrence funeral pyre and Quantrill knew what the message would say as soon as he saw the scout hurrying toward him. The Mount Oread patrol had spotted dust of approaching federal cavalry. Quantrill, not daring to face opposition even though he knew his force probably outnumbered them, gave the order to assemble and leave town. Quantrill saw he had done his job overly well and some of his raiders were too drunkenly eager for further bloodshed.

"We can't wait for them," Quantrill said. "They'll have to take their chances on getting away alone."

Scaggs was one of the stragglers. Determined to have one final fling before he followed the main group out of the city, he battered down the door of Fred Read's home. Mrs. Read was alone, A hungry glint lit up Scaggs' sweat-streaked face when he coupled the sight of the buxom women with the knowledge that Quantrill had already left town. Scaggs' lips curled back over tobacco-rotted teeth and he slowly stalked the woman huddling in terror in the corner of the bedroom.

With the tumult of gunfire and screams of pain and terror giving way to deathly stillness, Lawrence began to lick its gaping wounds. The alive and the near dead crawled from cellars, from under houses, out of wells, attics, even out of cesspools. A huge pall of smoke ballooned lazily into the sky.

Corpses were strewn everywhere, some scorched as they sprawled grotesquely near the flame-blackened hulks of stores. Winding black trails told where the wounded tried to crawl to safety. Often these trails ended with bodies. Above the crackling flames rose the deep-throated cries of women of all ages when they found the bodies of husbands, sons and brothers.

When William Speer reached home he found his mother in mournful shock, oblivious to her horribly burned hands and arms, suffered when she tried to save her home. She told William his brother was dead. Seething with burning frustration, the youth found an old rifle in the attic and raced for the south edge of Lawrence, hoping to meet a straggler. He did not have long to wait, for in a few minutes a lone rider galloped towards him. Speer fired at point blank range. The shot hit the guerrilla in the shoulder and knocked him from his horse.

Never having shot a man before, Speer stared stupidly at the injured guerrilla just as a Delaware Indian, a member of the advance force of counterattackers, reined up. The Indian dismounted and shot the raider through the heart, and in one swift swipe scalped him before hurrying on in hopes of adding to his dripping trophy. But Scaggs was the only guerrilla to fall in Lawrence that day.

The city was counting its dead when a sudden tumult from the south end of Lawrence caused heads to snap around and people to scream, "Quantrill's coming back!"

Townspeople started to run, only to stop short in profound horror when they saw a lone rider, a freedman, galloping toward them. Behind his horse churned clouds of dust as the scalped body of Larkin Scaggs was dragged from the end of a stout rope.

If Lawrence could never fully recover from Quantrill's outrage (Quantrill left 80 widows and 250 orphans in his wake, in addition to the $2,000,000 worth of burned and stolen property), neither would the United States Govern-

Quantrill's guerrillas depicted at the massacre and capture of Lawrence, Kansas. Quantrill left 80 widows and 250 orphans.

ment rest until it avenged the blasphemy. Fate began to turn against Quantrill and seeds of dissension sown by Anderson and Todd before the Lawrence massacre took root. Finally all that remained was a hard core of loyal followers and Katie Clark, a teenaged girl Quantrill had kidnaped and taught to be his wife without benefit of clergy. But nobody likes to be on the losing team, especially when the loser is wanted dead or alive, preferably the former, and Quantrill grumbled that Katie's favors were being bestowed much less frequently.

Union troops dogged Quantrill's trail when he fled Missouri into Kentucky and they finally caught up with him on May 10th, 1865, at a farm near Taylorsville where the guerrilla was sleeping in a hayloft. Taken by surprise, Quantrill ran across the barnyard. Shots criss-crossed and Quantrill was hit in the same spot he had shot so many unarmed men and boys — in the back. The bullet caromed off his left shoulder blade, sliced downward, severed his spinal cord and paralyzed him from his waist down. As he fell, another bullet cut off his right index finger.

Quantrill died 27 days later. He left all of his plunder to his mistress, and as one newspaper put it: "The only person who seems to have benefited by Quantrill's death is Katie Clark, who was bequeathed $2,000 in gold which she used to open a house of prostitution in St. Louis. At last reports she was doing prosperously well."

The Civil War naval battles of Hampton Roads off Norfolk and Newport News, Virginia, lasted only two days and ended with the famous fight between the ironclads *Monitor* and *Merrimac*. (Before conversion into an ironclad, the *Merrimac* was named *Virginia,* and some naval historians, especially those in the South, continue to refer to her by her original name.)

That was time enough to doom wooden warships, though Civil War buffs still argue about who won.

An Inside Look
At
The *Monitor* And
The *Merrimac*

The first clash of ironclads was long in the making but swift in its final drama.

At the beginning of the Civil War, the North had imposed a blockade of the Southern coast from Virginia to the Gulf States. By early January, 1862, the blockade's strength and effectiveness caused General Robert E. Lee to observe that "Wherever [the Union's] fleet can be brought, no opposition to his landing can be made. ... We have nothing to oppose to its heavy guns, which sweep over the low banks of this country with irresistible force."

In short, if the Confederacy didn't do something about the Union Navy, the war might take the course of Northern amphibious invasions anywhere in Southern coasts from Virginia to Texas. The dark shadow of this "ceaseless presence" also fell across the desk of Stephen R. Mallory, Secretary of the Confederate States Navy.

Mallory, a former U.S. Senator from Florida and Chairman of the Senate's Naval Affairs Committee, entered the Confederate government on March 20, 1861. He was well versed in advanced naval experiments. While still in Congress, he had written: "I regard the possession of an iron-armored ship as a matter of the first necessity. Such a vessel ... could traverse the entire coast, prevent all blockades, and encounter a fair prospect of success … Naval success dictates the wisdom and expediency of fighting with iron against wood."

Now, with only a fragmented Southern fleet to send against the Union's 100 steam and sailing frigates, brigs, sloops and other men-of-war, Mallory prepared to act on his earlier proposals for the U.S. Navy and build a fleet of ironclads to break the North's stronghold. As a start, two iron ships were to be built at New Orleans and Mobile.

A third would be made from the raised hulk of the old Union frigate *Merrimac*, lodging at Norfolk's navy yard. The federals had burned and scuttled her when evacuating Norfolk.

In a report of July 18, 1861, Mallory informed the Confederate War Department of his plans to convert the *Merrimac*, concluding: "As time is of the first consequence in this enterprise, I have not hesitated to commence the work and to ask Congress for the necessary appropriations."

By the middle of July, some 1,500 Southern workers in Norfolk were remodeling the *Merrimac*, while, at Richmond's Tredegar Iron Works, furnaces blazed night and day to supply the 1,000 tons of iron needed.

The mighty vessel was shaved down to within three and a half feet of her waterline. The live-oak hull, 275-feet-long, and 38-1/2-feet wide, was covered with a platform on which was centered a mound-shaped citadel, or superstructure, 160-feet-long and rounded at the ends.

The seven-foot-high sides of the structure were sloped at a 45-degree angle to deflect projectiles. Beneath a four-inch layer of iron plates covering the structure was an underlayer of 20-inch-thick heart pine and four inches of

Stephen R. Mallory, Secretary of the Confederate States Navy. To break the North's stronghold, he ordered the raised hulk of the Union frigate Merrimac *to be clad with 1,000 tons of iron by 1500 workers.*

The burning of the frigate Merrimac, *at the Gosport Navy Yard. She was raised from the bottom for transformation into the formidable ironclad of the celebrated battle with the* Monitor.

The Merrimac *undergoing her metamorphosis at the Gosport Navy Yard.*

oak. The deck atop the citadel was covered with iron grating for ventilation. Inside the superstructure were ten guns: a seven-inch Brooke rifle mounted on pivots at either end and, in each broadside, a six-inch Brooke and three nine-inch Dahlgren smoothbores.

Mounted at her prow was a massive iron ram to punch holes in the wooden sides of Union warships. Pig iron ballast was stowed in the hull to keep the *Merrimac* low enough in the water to put her guns in point-blank range of the wooden hulls and to put her ram several feet below their water level.

The *Merrimac's* original engines were retained in spite of several breakdowns. (They had been condemned, and she was in Norfolk awaiting new ones when war broke out.) The engineers converting her did what they could to repair them, but at best the engines could only manage five knots.

The activity in Norfolk and Richmond could not be kept a secret. Reports to Washington on an "infernal machine" being built that looked powerful enough to challenge the Union Navy were noted by Lincoln's War Department. But it was not until more detailed intelligence offered evidence of what Mallory was up to that Washington acted. On August 3, 1861, more than two months after construction on the *Merrimac* began, Congress directed U.S. Navy Secretary Gideon Welles to appoint a three-member board to investigate the feasibility of ironclads for the Union Navy.

In Richmond, Mallory learned of the Union action, but was not too concerned. The Northern board would consume time making its report and it should be many months after that before the U.S. Navy could launch an answer to the *Merrimac.* Meanwhile, work on his own ironclad surged ahead.

The three-man Union board obliged him even more.

Union Navy Secretary Gideon Welles, having learned about the Confederate Merrimac *project, appointed a board to look into the feasibility of ironclads for the North.*

After considering 15 types of proposed ironclads and one rubberclad ship, they finally settled on two conventional warships whose wooden sides would be girdled with iron. Congress appropriated funds to build them, and only an accident intervened to steer the Navy from what could have been a disastrous decision.

Cornelius S. Bushnell, of New Haven, was awarded one of the contracts for the two new wooden ships. He happened to show the design to John Ericsson, a Swedish immigrant inventor who was better known than respected in the Navy Department. Ericsson had designed the first screw-propelled warship for the Navy — the *U.S.S. Princeton*. During a demonstration of the *Princeton* for a presidential party in 1844 a cannon exploded. President John Tyler escaped injury, but Secretary of State Abel Upshur, Navy Secretary Thomas Gilmer and two Congressmen were killed.

Ericsson was not to blame for the accident, but he was tarred with the disaster and the Navy refused to pay him for his work. He sued, failed to collect, and became known as a troublemaker in the Navy Department. Some years later he built a model for an ironclad floating battery, and seven years before the Civil War, disdaining the U.S. Navy, he offered it to Napoleon III. Napoleon couldn't use it, but he was so impressed that he awarded Ericsson a medal for excellence.

At the start of the Civil War Ericsson had offered the same design to President Lincoln, but, getting no answer from the White House, he let the matter drop. Now, when Bushnell showed him his design for an iron-girdled conventional warship, Ericsson trotted out his cardboard model of the ironclad battery that had won him a French medal. Bushnell was impressed with the strange looking thing that

Captain John Ericsson, inventor of the Monitor. *After President Lincoln and Navy Secretary Welles had turned down his idea, Ericsson won them over with a two hour hard-sell presentation. The race was on to complete the* Monitor *before the* Merrimac *was ready.*

was later likened to a tin can on a shingle or a cheesebox on a raft. He borrowed the model and showed it to Navy Secretary Welles, who brought it to the attention of Lincoln and the three-man board.

After examining it, President Lincoln remarked, "all I have to say is what the girl said when she put her foot into the stocking. 'It strikes me there's something in it.'" The board, however, was certain it would capsize. Recalling the *Princeton* episode, they sent Bushnell on his way. "Take it home and worship it," Commander Charles H. Davis told him. "It will not be idolatry. It is in the image of nothing in the heaven above, or the earth beneath, or the waters under the earth."

But Bushnell persisted, and finally persuaded Welles and the board to hear Ericsson himself. On the morning of Sept. 13, 1861, Ericsson came to Welles' office and launched a two-hour defense of his floating iron battery. He was so persuasive that afterward Commodore Hiram Paulding, a member of the board, said to him, "I have learned more about the stability of a vessel from what you have said than I ever knew before."

By now the Navy Department had enough intelligence from Norfolk to feel that the Southern monster a-building there was genuine. They told Ericsson to go ahead, and they'd even name his craft the *Ericsson*. Start right away, they told him. The contract and the money would follow later.

The race to catch the *Merrimac* was on at last, amid a growing sense of alarm as more details of the Confederate ironclad flowed in.

The *Ericsson's* keel was laid on October 26, 1861. Ericsson's contract with the Navy specified that construction be completed within 100 working days, an almost impossible undertaking that he confidently accepted. She was launched on the 98th day, January 30, 1862.

Shortly before the launching, Ericsson suggested another name for the vessel: "This structure will admonish the leaders of the Southern Rebellion that the batteries on the banks of their rivers will no longer present barriers to the entrance of the Union forces. The ironclad intruder will thus prove a sever monitor to those leaders ... I propose to name the new battery *Monitor.*"

The bulk of the *Monitor* was built at the Continental Iron Works at the foot of Calyer Street in Brooklyn. The gun turret was built at a foundry appropriately called the Novelty Iron Works in New York. The iron plating came from the Albany Iron Works and smaller components from foundries as distant as Buffalo, N.Y., and Portsmouth, N.H.

The *Monitor* was 172-feet-long (103 feet shorter than the *Merrimac*) with a beam of 41-feet. The "raft" rose only about a foot above the water. It was encased in iron and supported by a lower hull 122-feet-long and 34-feet-wide. It drew 10 to 12 feet of water.

Mounted amidships was a circular turret 20-feet-in-diameter and nine-feet tall. The drum-shaped turret, encased in iron plates riveted together, formed a sandwich eight inches thick — twice that of the *Merrimac's* armor. Seated in a bronze ring inset in the deck, the turret rotated by means of a small steam engine. Although the *Merrimac* mounted ten guns, the *Monitor* carried but a pair of 11-inch Dahlgren smoothbores, sufficient, it was thought, to demolish the Rebel ship.

Fifty-five feet forward of the turret was the pilothouse, a squat box, three-and-a-half-feet-long, two-feet-eight-inches wide and slightly less than four-feet-high. Only the captain's and pilot's head and shoulders would be above deck and they would be protected by solid, nine-inch-thick blocks of wrought iron held together by three-inch bolts. A 5/8-inch slit was cut into the box. At 200 yards, it afforded a view 80-feet-high. (Against Ericsson's protests, and with subsequent near-fatal results, the slit was widened to about one inch.) The battery's twin steam boilers were mounted aft under a collapsible smokestack. Air was sucked in through deck vents.

Confederate spies were busy learning all this about the *Monitor*. Their work was considerably simplified when Ericsson, goaded by recurrent criticism of his contract, supplied the *Scientific American* magazine with complete details and drawings of his battery. A rebel spy urged that the *Merrimac's* ram should be lengthened to sink the *Monitor*. The Southern ship's ram was, accordingly, extended out to four-feet — a blunder as it would turn out.

The *Monitor's* 56-man crew was selected from Navy volunteers. Her commander, Lieutenant John Worden, was 44 and had held his rank for 20 years. He had yet to command his own ship. He had just been released from an Alabama prisoner of war camp and, although ailing, was known for his courage. He had requested the *Monitor* assignment before her keel was laid.

The 350-man crew of the *Merrimac* was recruited from army volunteers, since there were few men in the Confederacy with previous sea experience. Mallory appointed as skipper the 62-year-old founder of the Naval Academy at Annapolis, Franklin Buchanan. A Navy veteran of 47 years, Buchanan resigned his commission in 1861 when it appeared that his native Maryland would secede. Later, he

Lt. John Worden, 44, just released from a Confederate prisoner of war camp, was given command of the 56 man Monitor's crew. He had requested the assignment before her keel was laid.

Commodore Franklin Buchanan, 62-year-old founder of the Naval Academy at Annapolis, was appointed skipper of the Confederate's Merrimac, *and commanded her 350 men.*

The launching of the Monitor *at Green Point, Brooklyn, February, 1862.*

withdrew his resignation, but Secretary Welles refused him and the elderly Buchanan went south.

In spite of Mallory's confidence that the U.S. Navy could not produce a challenger for the *Merrimac* in time to save the fleet at Hampton Roads, the *Monitor* was turned over to the government on February 25, 1862, a few weeks before the completion of the *Merrimac*. On Thursday, March 6, 1862, following orders from Secretary of War Edwin Stanton in Washington, who feared it might already be too late to stop the *Merrimac*, she sailed for Newport News.

The *Merrimac* was completed on March 5, 1862. Three days later, she left her haven in the Elizabeth River and headed for Newport News and its Union fleet.

Anchored under the protection of the federal fortifications at Newport News was a fleet of about a dozen wooden-hulled Union ships and gunboats. Altogether they mounted more than 200 guns and effectively blockaded the entrance to Norfolk and Richmond. Mightiest of the blockaders was the 30-gun *Cumberland*, a sailing sloop-of-war which lay 30 yards off Newport Point. Strung out in a line east of her were the frigate *Congress*, with 50 guns; and two sister frigates of the old *Merrimac*: the 47-gun *Minnesota* and the 46-gun

The Merrimac, *from a sketch made the day before the battle.*

Roanoke. Lastly was the *St. Lawrence,* a 52-gun frigate. Beyond these ships lay five gunboats.

For months their crews had heard reports of the Rebel ironclad, but nobody had seen her and it was beginning to appear as if no one ever would.

March 8 dawned clear and mild and gave promise of being a dreary repetition of other days during the endless months that had passed. The tedium was broken only by the knowledge that this was laundry day. By mid-morning, the rigging of the *Cumberland* and the other ships was hung with freshly-laundered clothing flapping in the breeze. Many aboard the *Cumberland* dove overboard for a morning swim before the noon mess call. If life had become lethargic for them, at least they were eating well. The fare aboard the *Cumberland* that Saturday was roast beef. For more than 100 of her crew, it was to be their final meal.

Forty minutes past the noon hour, the lookout aboard the small support steamship *Mount Vernon* noticed a plume of black smoke moving from Norfolk. The *Mount Vernon* hoisted Signal No. 551: "Coming enemy vessel is." Five minutes passed. The *Mount Vernon's* officers watched for an acknowledgement from the *Cumberland* and the frigates. None came. They fired a shot in the direction of the smoke. Still no response from the other ships. Not until 1:10 p.m. — half an hour after the signal flag was raised — did the *Roanoke* finally acknowledge.

By now the smoke could be seen coming from a stack aft of a most peculiar looking vessel. The lookout raised his glass for a better look. The *Merrimac!* The alarm was quickly relayed among the fleet. Laundry was hauled in, drummers beat to quarters, the ships cleared for action and the guns were run out.

Meanwhile, the *Merrimac* was proving "as unmanageable as a water-logged vessel." Four men struggled with her wheel. Because of her deep draft, Buchanan had purposely timed his attack for the 1:40 p.m. high tide.

Calling his crew of former soldiers together. Buchanan said: "Sailors, in a few minutes you will have the long-looked-for opportunity of showing your devotion to our cause. Remember that you are about to strike for your country and your homes. The Confederacy expects every man to do his duty ... and you shall not complain that I do not take you in close enough. Go to your guns!"

At ten minutes past 2 o'clock, the sluggish *Merrimac* crawled past the *Congress*, which opened with a solid shot from her stern gun. "It glanced off her forward casement like a drop of water from a duck's back," a crewman later wrote. The *Cumberland*, realizing she was the *Merrimac's* prey, blazed away. The frigates *Minnesota* and *St. Lawrence* made ready to join the battle, but for some unexplained reason, both moved too close to shore and went aground. They were out of the fight. The *Roanoke*, laid up with a broken propeller shaft, was towed by tugs to within range but her shots were ineffective. Land batteries and gunboats opened fire. Still the silent *Merrimac* bore in, thick black smoke shuffling from her stack. At one time, 100 guns were firing at her, but the Rebel seemed oblivious to the hail of shot and shell.

The Merrimac was now in easy range and the *Cumberland's* crew saw her forward gunport flip up and the ugly muzzle of the Brooke 7-inch flash flame. The shell tore into the *Cumberland's* bulwarks. Exploding amidships, it slaughtered nine Marines. Again the Brooke rifle boomed. This time the *Cumberland's* forward pivot gun was knocked out and its entire crew was killed or maimed. Both of Gun Captain John Kirker's arms were sliced off at the shoulder sockets and as he was being carried below he begged shipmates to cut his throat.

Now, slithering through the shot-and-shell-pocked water, her forward deck awash, the *Merrimac* drove her four-foot ram deep into the *Cumberland's* hull "like a knife cutting into a watermelon." Buchanan immediately signaled for all engines to reverse and the *Merrimac* backed off. As it came away, the 1500-pound ram stayed embedded in the *Cumberland.* Some water entered the hole in the *Merrimac's* open prow. The ram had, however, opened the *Cumberland's* side "wide enough to drive in a horse and cart." With survivors leaping over the sides she sank bow first into nine fathoms of water.

The guns of the other Union ships redoubled their efforts. Broadside upon broadside whanged against the *Merrimac's* sloping citadel, but most of the shots merely ricocheted and made water geysers in the oyster beds a mile away. Some shots did find the target. Two of the *Merrimac's* guns were shattered; her boats were shot away, along with stanchions and the flagstaff. The Confederate flag had to be remounted atop a boarding pike. A shell exploded in her stack and the shattering roar made the Union gun crews cheer. They though the *Merrimac's* boiler had blown and the rebel was finished. She was taking on water where her ram had been and was even now heading up the James River, apparently in flight. The *Congress'* crews began to secure her guns.

What they could not know was that the *Merrimac,* except for the loss of her stinger, was as deadly as ever. Because of her poor maneuverability and speed, she re-

The U.S.S. Cumberland goes down victim of the Merrimac. A wooden ship up against an ironclad had little chance.

Library of Congress Photo

When the flames on the burning USS Congress *reached her powder magazines, the explosion ripped the frigate in half.* The Merrimac *had claimed her first victim.*

quired time to turn around and she sought the safety of distance to do so. Thirty minutes later, the *Merrimac* came about and headed straight for the stern of the *Congress*, whose crews were hurriedly piped back to their guns. Admiral Buchanan permitted himself a moment to reflect that his brother was paymaster aboard the *Congress* before his gunners zeroed in and blitzed the wooden frigate, which replied as best she could. "Our shot had apparently no effect upon her," reported an officer aboard the *Congress*, "but the result of her broadside on our ship was simply terrible. One of her shells dismounted an 8-inch gun and either killed or wounded everyone of the gun's crew, while the slaughter at the other guns was fearful." Among the fallen was her Captain, Joseph B. Smith.

The *Congress* ran up a white flag. When Buchanan climbed to the promenade deck atop the *Merrimac's* citadel to oversee removal of the injured, a fusillade of sniper fire opened from the shore. A minié ball shattered his thigh. The command of the *Merrimac* now fell upon Buchanan's young executive officer, Lt. Catesby ap Jones.

Buchanan gave his final order for the *Congress*: "Pour hot shot into her and don't leave her until she's afire. They must look after their own wounded, since they won't let us." By twilight, the *Congress* was ablaze. The *Merrimac* started after the grounded *Minnesota*, but she was saved by the ebbing tide. Lieutenant Jones, heeding his pilot's urging, returned the *Merrimac* to the haven of the Elizabeth River before it, too, grounded, Tomorrow was another day.

Secretary Mallory was ecstatic when news of the victory reached Richmond. He envisioned the *Merrimac* steaming up the Potomac and lobbing shells into President Lincoln's bedroom before going on to attack New York and the Brooklyn Navy Yard.

President Lincoln, meanwhile, called his Cabinet into emergency nighttime session. He was stunned by the disastrous news of the slaughter of 300 men and the loss of two ships by the ironclad *Merrimac.* Certainly, Gen. George McClellan's long-planned Peninsular Campaign against Richmond could not start while the Rebel threat remained. War Secretary Stanton was all for sending word to New York and Boston to prepare the defend themselves against the *Merrimac.* What answer could they possibly provide? The *Monitor,* they decided, would have to bypass Newport News and sail to Washington to protect the Capital. Appropriate orders were drawn.

At 9 o'clock that night, the *Monitor* chugged into Hampton Roads. Her arrival stirred little interest. The thousands of people lining the hills to watch the *Congress* burn barely noticed her. Among them was McKean Buchanan, who, unlike his brother commanding the *Merrimac,* had escaped from the *Congress* unwounded.

Lieutenant Worden and his crew aboard the *Monitor* were hardly prepared for the tragic news that greeted them in the Roads. The voyage south had been hell and the *Monitor* had come close to sinking in the foul weather. Water had poured in onto her fires and many of her crew had collapsed from the coal gas. The others had pumped and bailed and had gone sleepless for 48 hours. Seasick, they had eaten little.

Reviewing the situation that evening, the naval command in Newport News agreed to put aside the orders deploying the *Monitor* to Washington. She would, instead, stand by the *Minnesota* and keep the *Merrimac* away if she could.

The somber mood on the Union side was further

darkened early in the morning when flames finally reached the *Congress'* powder magazines. The jolting explosion ripped the frigate in half.

Dawn of Sunday, March 9, 1862, promised another clear, cloudless day. Off toward Newport News the hulk of the *Congress* still smoldered and the calm waters of Hampton Roads were peppered with flotsam and gory reminders of the preceding day's battle.

Shortly after 8 o'clock, the *Merrimac*, with the hole in her prow plugged and her smokestack patched, once again came lumbering into Hampton Roads. The grotesque floating barn with her stack puffing thick black smoke headed for the still-grounded *Minnesota*. And now the outlandish Union cheesebox-on-a-raft churned out to intercept the Rebel, while thousands of Virginians brought picnic lunches and camp stools and gathered along the hilltops to watch the naval battle of the century.

Historians differ on the exact sequence of events between 9 a.m. and noon that day, and the subsequent recollections of various crewmen of the *Monitor* and *Merrimac* were written long after the battle. It is agreed that the *Merrimac* opened with a 150-pound, 10-inch shell fired at the *Minnesota*. It fell short. For the time, the *Minnesota* was spared further bombardment as the *Monitor* moved in.

In her turret, Samuel Dana Greene, the executive officer, had the sensation of being encased in a big black drum. What light there was came from the iron grating across the top of the turret. It cast a crazy-quilt pattern of shadows over him and his gun crew, which was standing ready by the side-by-side pair of 11-inch Dahlgrens.

John Lorimer Worden, aboard the Monitor, *gave the command, "Commerce firing!"*

Minutes passed before Worden gave the command: "Commence firing!"

The gun crew opened the heavy portstopper and Greene got his first sight of the *Merrimac*. It was only 50 yards dead ahead. An easy shot. Greene yanked the lockstring and the Dahlgren boomed a direct hit which ricocheted off the sloping citadel. The portstopper slammed shut and the other one was tugged open. The second shot also clanged harmlessly off the Rebel.

Peering through the pilothouse slit, Worden cursed the negligible effect and swore at the Navy Department's insistence upon 15-pound charges, rather than the 30-pounders which certainly would have poked holes in the Rebel. The overly-cautious Admiral John Dahlgren had thought the *Monitor's* untried guns might explode with the heavier powder charge, a groundless fear it was later found.

The *Merrimac* answered with a 150-pound shell. Its bullet-nose scooped a perfect mold, four-inches deep, in the turret before exploding. Acting Master L.N. Stodder was bracing his knee against the wall of the turret as he operated the steam engine that turned it. He was knocked unconscious by the impact. But the turret had withstood the hit and the rotating mechanism was not damaged.

As the *Monitor* came around to the stern of the *Merrimac*, Worden ordered Greene to aim for the Rebel's exposed propeller and rudder. Steam hissed and the turret rotated. The portstopper was opened and Greene got off a shot that slammed to one side of the turret. Two feet in the other direction and the *Merrimac* would have been helpless. Greene would not get a better chance, and he could hardly be blamed for his inaccurate fire. Cooped up in the rotating turret, he soon became disoriented and could not know his aft from his forward, his port from his starboard. White chalk marks made on the deck below the turret to indicate these directions were obliterated early in the battle by the gunners' feet.

"When a gun was ready for firing," Greene later explained, "The turret would be started on its revolving journey in search of the target, and when found it was taken 'on the fly' because the turret could not accurately be controlled."

In addition to the slow-to-start, slow-to-stop turret, other problems soon arose. The clumsy, hard-to-open port-stoppers, and the time consumed in passing along the heavy shot up into the turret, prevented the *Monitor* from getting off shots oftener than one every seven minutes. The *Merrimac*, on the other hand, was getting off two or more to every one of the *Monitor's*.

The problems worsened when the concussion from

Confederate seamen load Merrimac's big *guns, but the projectiles only dented* Monitor's *hull.*

one of the *Merrimac's* shots smashed the speaking tube. The Paymaster and the Captain's Clerk were then positioned along the passageway and relayed Worden's commands. But the turret had to be turned until its bottom opening lined up with that in the deck before Greene could find out what the Captain had in mind.

Nor did the *Monitor* have any monopoly on the tactical and design blunders. The *Merrimac* carried only shell and grape shot, sufficient to tear into wooden hulls but ineffective against the *Monitor's* iron body. The bobbing turret of the *Monitor* offered only a 9-by-20-foot target — and many of the *Merrimac's* shots missed. Too, the *Merrimac's* shell-shattered smokestack was so shot up that "a flock of pigeons could have flown through it." The sieve-like stack was making it difficult to keep a draught in the furnaces. The below-deck areas were filling with smoke and coal gas, making the engineers and gunners groggy.

"On our gun deck was bustle, smoke, grimy figures and stern commands," Chief Engineer Ashton Ramsay of the *Merrimac* later recalled, "while down in the engine and boiler rooms the sixteen furnaces were belching out fire and smoke. ... The noise of the cracking, roaring fires, escaping steam, and the loud and labored pulsations of the engines, together with the roar of battle above and the thud and vibration of the huge masses of iron which were hurled against us produced a scene and sound to be compared only with the poet's picture of the lower regions." Concussions from the *Monitor's* blasts brought blood streaming from the noses and ears of the Rebel's crew.

As the morning wore on, the *Merrimac* and the *Monitor* steamed in opposite circles. The *Monitor* got off its shots when the circles impinged. The *Merrimac* thundered with

Artist's conceptions of the battle in progress.

broadside after meaningless broadside. Wrote the *Minnesota's* captain. G. J. Van Brunt: "Gun after gun was fired by the *Monitor*, which was returned with whole broadsides, with no more effect (on either) than so many pebblestones thrown by a child."

Suddenly, the *Merrimac* scraped bottom and came to a dead stop. Aground, her rudder and propeller offered a stationary target. Jones called for full steam to get her off. Chief Engineer Ramsay fastened down the safety valves while the engineroom crew stuffed the furnaces with oily rags, wood chips, anything that would burn faster than coal. Smoke gushed from her stack and filled the engineroom. Her propeller churned the water to a muddy mush as the *Monitor* and the *Minnesota* and their consorts whaled away for 20 minutes without crippling that vital area. Finally, the *Merrimac* freed herself.

If the Rebel shells could not harm the *Monitor*, then perhaps the *Merrimac* could ram her to the bottom, a tactic which could cost the *Merrimac* too. Signaling for a full head of steam, Jones sent the *Merrimac* at the *Monitor*. But the cumbersome Rebel only succeeded in getting close enough to nudge the *Monitor* and put a small dent in her side.

The 20-minute volley against the grounded *Merrimac* had depleted the *Monitor's* ammunition. Greene got off one last shot, which merely zinged off the *Merrimac's* iron. Then he headed back to port to reload. Assuming that the *Monitor* had tasted enough, Jones lost no time. He ordered the *Merrimac's* helm put over and she pulled across the placid water toward the *Minnesota*. Her first shell gouged a gaping hole in the frigate and wiped out four staterooms. Jones bored in for the kill.

The *Minnesota* trained every one of her 47 guns on the rebel and let loose with a broadside blizzard of shot and shell which merely bounced off the *Merrimac*. More than any other incident of this day's battle, these few minutes were to be regarded by many as the last hurrah for the age of wooden warships.

To Jones' surprise, the *Monitor* suddenly reappeared. Again the ironclads closed and again the *Merrimac's* shot glanced harmlessly off the turret while the *Monitor's* did only minor damage to the Rebel's plates. Jones tried a new tactic. If the enemy's turret was impenetrable, perhaps he could knock out the *Monitor* by concentrating his fire on her pilothouse.

At 11:30 a.m., as the *Monitor* came around the *Merrimac's* stern, the *Merrimac's* Brooke rifle fired.

Executive Officer Greene's first inkling that something was wrong came when, within the turret, he heard the *Monitor's* engines throbbing strong and felt her surge forward. Then he heard yells coming from below. He was being called to the pilothouse by Captain Worden's men there. Green was horrified at what he saw when he got there. Blood was gushing "from every pore in Worden's face." The shot had struck the front of the wheelhouse as Worden peered through the slit, which had been widened against Ericsson's protests. Shards of iron and bits of powder had peppered and blinded Worden. He was suffering from a severe concussion, as was the helmsman who, in his daze, had permitted the *Monitor* to bolt upstream. Although Worden ultimately recovered, one entire side of his face was forever powder-blackened.

Seeing the *Monitor* aimlessly churning away from the

As Worden peered through the slit in the wheelhouse, a shell from the Merrimac's *Brooke* rifle struck near the slit, blinding him. Blood gushed from "every pore in his face," and he suffered a severe concussion.

Part of the crew of the Monitor *from a photograph taken shortly after the battle.*

fight, Jones once more assumed that the Union ironclad was vanquished and he turned the *Merrimac* back toward the *Minnesota.*

Jones was eager to continue the fight, but, as on the previous day, the *Merrimac's* pilot now advised him that the tide was ebbing and there was danger of being grounded again. The *Merrimac,* Jones noted, was also low on ammunition. He ordered the ship returned to Norfolk.

Worden, meanwhile, relinquished command of the *Monitor* to the 22-year-old Greene, who brought her around once more to do battle. Greene was astonished to see that the *Merrimac* was heading for Norfolk. He was tempted to pursue her, but the Monitor's order were to protect the Minnesota, and that did not mean chasing the *Merrimac* into Norfolk.

The battle was over, a draw. But in those brief hours, the navies of the world were made obsolete.

Each side claimed victory, and historians today argue the outcome. The murderous *Merrimac* sank two Union warships and damaged another. Their crew were decimated. And McClellan's plan to take Richmond by advancing up the York Peninsula was hampered by the presence of the *Merrimac*. But the *Monitor* had checked her. If her sting was not completely removed, she did no further major harm. The Northern blockade was still as effective as ever, and the North had the time and the potential to build a fleet of ironclads. The South had neither.

The *Merrimac* and the *Monitor* sparred several times during the next weeks, but neither side was willing to risk the loss of its lone ironclad in a rematch by venturing into the other's domain. For a while the *Merrimac* stood guard over the James River and the *Monitor* over Chesapeake Bay, but both ships had little time left.

After Norfolk was evacuated on May 8, 1862, the *Merrimac*, unable to escape up the James, was burned to prevent her from falling into Union hands. The *Monitor* saw some action later, none of it particularly notable. Then, on New Year's Eve, 1862, while being towed to Charleston, S.C., to support the fleet, she was caught in a gale. Heavy seas swamped her and she went down off Cape Hatteras with 16 of her crew.

The naval warships that were built after the encounter of the *Monitor* and the *Merrimac* all bore the mark of this famous battle, which tolled the eclipse of wooden ships from the world's great navies.

John Ericsson lived to be 85. In 1926, in recognition of his work on the Monitor, and on naval guns, torpedoes and

After battling the Merrimac *to a draw, the Monitor sank in a gale on December 19, 1862.*

submarines, he became one of the earliest foreign private citizens to be honored on a U.S. postage stamp. Shortly after his death in 1889, his remains were carried to Sweden for burial in his native land. The *U.S.S. Baltimore*, an all steel warship, took him home for his final rest.

The incredible story of the most desperate mission of the Civil War. In 1864 Lieutenant William Barker Cushing crossed into Confederate territory with a crude torpedo. He was determined to get revenge.

Lt. Cushing's Revenge

The autumn night was ominously black. A persistent rain pattered upon the decks of the Union gunboat *Shamrock* and the two steam launches it was mothering in the Albemarle Sound off Rebel-held Plymouth, North Carolina. Nervously eager to be on his way, Lieutenant William Barker Cushing quickly finished his last minute inspection of the launches, the crude torpedo rigged to a spar on the side of one of them and the 15 heavily armed volunteers he would lead on a desperate mission deep into Confederate territory.

Then the 21-year-old lieutenant gave the signal to cast off and the two boats chugged softly away from the *Shamrock*. They pointed their bows towards the mouth of the Roanoke River that would carry them up to Plymouth and the Rebel ram *Albemarle* named after the body of water the Confederates soon hoped to clear of the Union gunboats that now blockaded it.

Cushing's boyishly delicate features did not quite mask his impatient determination, verging upon insane desire, to destroy the Confederate ironclad and settle a longstanding personal grudge. Cushing and his raiders were aware that this mission would probably be a one-way trip, and nobody with dependents was allowed to volunteer for it.

In a few hours the launches entered the Roanoke which averaged a mere 150 yards wide.

"Now, remember," Cushing whispered, "not another word is to be spoken from here on in. Not even a whisper."

Cushing's raiders hardly needed the warning. They

knew the tree-lined banks were saturated with dozens of Rebel sentries. It would be miraculous if Cushing ever got within hailing distance of the *Albemarle*, what with underwater chains and other obstructions tuned to sound an alarm if an intruding boat's hull scraped them. Even less were Cushing's chances of squeaking past the sunken Union gunboat *Southfield*, a mile below Plymouth. The gunboat's hurricane deck crawled with Rebel pickets ready to fire warning rockets if the Union tried to attack the ram from the river.

Softly, like cats stalking a mouse, the two boats wormed their way eight miles up the Roanoke. In the oppressive silence heavy with tension, Lieutenant Cushing remembered the words he had written his cousin a few weeks earlier: "I am going to have a vote of thanks from Congress, or six feet of pine box by the next time you hear from me."

For six frustrating months the Federal flotilla had tried in every conceivable way to sink the Confederate ironclad which had dealt them such a humiliating blow when Plymouth was recaptured by the Rebels in April.

The strategic port's fall began when the ram drove its cast iron prow into the wooden hull of the *Southfield* and routed four other Union gunboats guarding the vulnerable river side of Plymouth's fortifications. The fight also cost the North one of its best officers — Lieutenant Commander Charles W. Flusser, leader of the flotilla. Flusser was killed by ricocheting fragments of a shell that bounced off the ironclad's sloping sides. Ironically, the shot which disemboweled Flusser was fired from an 11-inch Dahlgren aboard his own boat.

The Union debacle at Plymouth was one that presaged immediate retaliation. But the Yankee anger that promised revenge was as nothing compared to the wrath seething inside Cushing when he learned of Flusser's death; for together they had won fame as a fighting team and were the closest of friends.

Cushing vowed to all within hearing: "I shall never rest until I avenge Flusser's death."

That he more than fulfilled his promise was told by a chronicler who afterwards wrote: "Flusser was avenged in a manner so complete and so terrible that the entire world paused to contemplate it as the greatest act of personal bravery in the annals of naval warfare." Cushing was conceded the unenviable title of "Most Shot at Man in the Navy" and was called "The hero of the war" by no less than Admiral David G. Farragut.

Cushing's determination for revenge became even more compulsive two weeks after the loss of Plymouth. Then nine sleek federal gunboats bore down double file upon the ram when it steamed defiantly into the sound. The Union hammered the Rebel *Albemarle* with more than 300 shots that afternoon, but the shells pinged harmlessly off the indifferent iron turtle's thick shell. This failing, the North tried to ram the *Albemarle*; they tried to torpedo her and they futilely attempted to foul the ironclad's propellers with a fishing seine.

Four hours after the fight began, the ram triumphantly shuffled back to Plymouth, leaving in its wake the sinking *Wyalusing* and the badly crippled *Sassacus* which had swallowed a cannon ball that popped open its boilers. Spewing steam had savagely scalded 20 of its crew.

The *Albemarle*, content to rest upon its laurels, and realizing that any further attempt to engage the federal flotilla might result in disaster, never again ventured out from Plymouth.

Admiral David G. Farragut called Cushing "The hero of the war."

Admiral Lee, almost desperately ready to snatch upon any reed that would destroy the Rebel menace, listened intently when Lieutenant Cushing suggested two plans. The first, which the cocky lieutenant admitted he didn't favor, called for 100 men to carry rubber rafts through the swamps to within several hundred yards of the *Albemarle*. Early in the morning, while the Confederates dozed, Cushing and his men would inflate the rafts, board the ram and take her captive.

"Now that's one possibility," said Cushing, omitting the "sir," a courtesy he often overlooked even during his Annapolis days. "My second plan, while more hazardous, is better. I'll outfit two open launches — each about 30 feet long with small engines — arm then with a 12-pound howitzer in their bows and rig a swivel boom on the starboard side. On the end of the boom I'll fasten a torpedo, like a spear. Then, under cover of darkness, I'll go up the Roanoke to Plymouth. ..."

Noting the look of incredulity that came over the Admiral's face, Cushing quickly explained, "That's the most dangerous and best protected passage. Consequently the Rebs might not be expecting an attack from that direction and I'll catch them by surprise.

"When I reach the *Albemarle* I'll dash in with one of my boats while the other stands off to cover me with the howitzer. If my attempt fails, they can make a stab at it."

As Cushing went into greater detail on this plan, Admiral Lee gazed deeply into the young officer's clear, grayish-blue eyes. They seemed almost obsessed with Cushing's insane hatred for the *Albemarle* and his whole body seemed to vibrate.

Cushing's smooth-shaven chin, his baby-faced innocence and his straight dark hair certainly did not bespeak the hell-for-leather reputation he enjoyed. But, thought the admiral, if anyone can pull off such a suicidal stunt it would be this colorful young officer.

Cushing, after serving as a page boy in the House of Representatives, was appointed to Annapolis. While not a poor student scholastically, Cushing's chief claim to fame at the academy was his amazing ability to pile up demerits.

The student midshipman's propensity for practical jokes finally provided the straw that broke the collective faculty's back. During Cushing's senior year he drew an impish caricature of his Spanish instructor who was overly sensitive about being nipped by a horse. The incident caused the staid officers at Annapolis to decide that Cushing might be happier pursuing some other career. Only their wording was little less diplomatic when they summarized his record: "General conduct bad; aptitude for naval service not good; not recommended for continuance at the Academy." Two weeks after Cushing was permitted to resign, the Rebels fired upon Fort Sumter and the Civil War was on in earnest.

President Lincoln's call for volunteers was quickly answered by Cushing who regarded secession as a personal affront and a glorious chance for adventure. After considerable debate, the Navy Department accepted Cushing as an Acting Midshipman, but only after he made a personal promise of honorable conduct to Secretary of the Navy Gideon Welles.

Admiral Lee, after hearing Cushing out, gave his consent to the second plan and sent the young Lieutenant under secret orders to Washington where Assistant Navy Secretary Gustavus Fox gave his pessimistic consent to the project. Cushing got two launches in New York and started back for Albemarle Sound, only to lose one of his boats in a

Cushing, a former page boy in the House of Representatives, was asked to resign from the Naval Academy at Annapolis because of poor behavior. His resignation became effective two weeks before Ft. Sumter was fired upon, beginning the War Between The States. The Navy quickly accepted him back when the war broke out.

storm. Undaunted, he decided to proceed against the ram with only one torpedo launch.

When Cushing reached the flotilla, the air tingled with excitement as officers and men realized that major mission was in the offing. They guessed it was an assault against the *Albemarle* even before the call for volunteers went out.

That night Cushing made his first attempt to storm the Roanoke. Hardly had he set out, however, when a Union tug heard the chugging of his launch's engine. Cushing immediately turned back and the next day carpenters boxed in the motor to muffle its telltale sound.

Luckily, Cushing learned that same day the Rebels had 25 pickets stationed aboard the sunken *Southfield*. This new obstacle decided Cushing to take along a second cutter borrowed from one of the gunboats. Its purpose would be to capture the pickets, or at least divert their attention while Cushing steered for the ram.

At 8:30 the night of October 27, 1864, Cushing set out for Plymouth. Entering enemy waters he tied ropes around his hands and legs and with them directed the helmsman while he knelt in the bow. The other boat crept silently behind.

Then they sighted the *Southfield*. There was no sign of life aboard her, but Cushing knew she bristled with sharpshooters. Pelting rain, though it chilled Cushing and his raiders, helped to drown out the engine mutterings. Cushing motioned for the other launch to come alongside.

"They haven't seen us," he whispered. "Let's not take the risk that they'll get off a rocket before you overpower them. I planned to destroy the *Albemarle*, but now I think she'd make a good prize. We'll both go after her.

"I know how Plymouth is laid out. There's a wharf a little below the *Albemarle*. We'll land there, creep around to the landside of the ram, and board her from the river bank where she least expects attack. Let the land batteries throw at us what they will; we'll sail the *Albemarle* right out into the sound. We'll be protected by iron of the Reb's own making!"

In a few minutes Cushing was within hailing distance of the ram. Seemingly asleep, the *Albemarle* looked like a great iron alligator wallowing in the muck along the shore. But the ram wasn't dozing. At that instant Cushing's chain of good luck snapped.

"Halt! Who goes there?" bawled a picket aboard the ram. Cushing ignored the command and whispered an order for the second launch to hurry back to the *Southfield* to try to keep an avenue of escape open. But it was too late.

The *Albemarle* sprang to life. On shore the garrison raced to battle stations. The control of Plymouth depended upon continued protection by the ram. Not having the slightest idea of what they were shooting at, or even whether the sentry only thought he had heard something, the shore batteries and the ram's Armstrong pivot guns peppered the darkness with a storm of lead.

On shore the Confederates ignited a gigantic bonfire, hoping to silhouette this unknown intruder afloat in the river. The fire helped the Rebels, but it was a godsend to Cushing.

As his torpedo boat knifed across the waters, Cushing squinted into the quivering glow of the flames. Suddenly he swallowed hard. A few yards ahead of him was an obstacle he had totally forgotten to take into consideration.

A ring of hefty cypress logs encircled the *Albemarle* for

The ironclad ram Albemarle *seemed invincible, even to torpedos.*

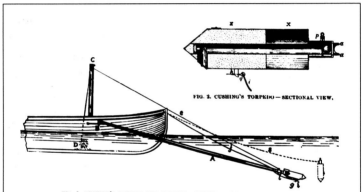

FIG. 2. CUSHING'S TORPEDO — SECTIONAL VIEW.

FIG. 1. CUSHING'S LAUNCH AND TORPEDO — SHOWING METHODS OF WORKING.

A long spar A (Fig. 1) was pivoted by means of a universal joint on its inboard end into the bracket B, the bracket being securely fastened to the outside of the boat. The spar was raised or lowered by means of a halliard e, which passed through a block at the head of the stanchion C, and thence down to the drum of a small windlass D, situated in the bottom of the boat, directly abaft the stanchion. On the outboard end of the spar was a socket, or head, which carried the shell. The shell was held in place only by a small pin g, which passed through a lug h, protruding from the lower side of the shell, and thence through an inclined plane i, which was attached to the socket. The lug and pin are clearly shown in Fig. 2. To detach the shell the pin g was pulled, and the shell forced gently out of the socket. This was accomplished by a lanyard f, which led from the boat to the head of the socket, passing back of the head of the shell through the lugs a a, so that when the lanyard was tautened it would force the shell out. A smaller lanyard l, leading to the pin g, was spliced to the lanyard f in such a manner that when the lanyard f was pulled, first the pin and then the shell would come out.

The shell (Fig. 2) contained an air chamber X and a powder chamber E. The result of this arrangement was that when the shell was detached it assumed a vertical position, with the air chamber uppermost, and, being lighter than its volume of water, it floated gradually toward the surface. At the top of its central shaft or tube was a grape-shot, held in place by a pin p, to which was attached the lanyard s. The pin was a trigger, and the lanyard was known as the trigger-line. Upon pulling the lanyard the pin came out, the shot fell by its own weight upon the nipple, which was covered by a percussion-cap and connected directly with the powder chamber, whereupon the torpedo exploded.

When the spar was not in use it was swung around by means of a stern line, bringing the head of the spar to the stern of the boat. To use the apparatus, the shell was put in place and the spar was swung around head forward; it was then lowered by means of the halliard e to the required depth; the lanyard f was pulled, withdrawing the pin g, and forcing out the shell; finally, when the floating shell had risen to its place, the trigger-line s was pulled and the torpedo fired.

Diagram and explanation of Cushing's torpedo from Battles And Leaders Of The Civil War.

a good 30 feet out from the hull. No torpedo could possibly bulldoze its way through that barrier. Cushing's men also saw the bulwark jutting a few inches above water. They felt a sickening sensation as they looked up into the muzzles of two pivot guns and realized they were about to die without seeing their mission completed.

"Put her about!" Cushing signaled, jerking a rope. The torpedo launch sheered off and steamed out into the river. Then he played his last trump card. When Cushing was 100 yards out he turned his launch around and raced full speed for the *Albemarle*. The water around him churned with grapeshot. Cushing felt the back of his coat vanish. A shell fragment sliced off the sole of his shoe as he knelt in the bow.

An instant later Cushing's launch crashed into the cypress logs. The tiny boat leapfrogged into the air and over the hurdle, slapping down upon the slimy water inside the ring. The abrupt impact nearly spilled Cushing and his men from the launch. Now it glided slowly towards the *Albemarle*. Cushing looked up into the yawning mouth of the pivot gun, less than 10 feet from his head. Cushing's howitzer belched again, spoiling the aim of the *Albemarle's* gunners. Their shot sizzled harmlessly a scant few inches over his head.

Cushing signaled for the boom to be lowered as the launch inched closer to the ram. The forward motion now brought the stubby torpedo under the ram's overhang. A bullet tore off a chunk of flesh from Cushing's left hand. He tugged at the detaching line. The torpedo plopped into the water. A moment later it bobbed to the surface. Cushing jerked another line, withdrawing a small pin. A two-inch ball pinged upon the percussion cap and touched off the 60-pound charge of powder.

If the explosion's flash was blinding, doubly so was

Cushing's homemade torpedo strikes home, as the Albemarle *explodes.*

the 100-pound grape broadside that vomited from the ram. The *Albemarle's* shot scooped up an enormous wave of water that swamped the launch.

"Every man for himself!" boomed Cushing.

His men leaped overboard. Cushing threw his sword and revolver into the river. Then ripping off his shot-shredded jacket and shoes, he dove into the water just as the Rebels put out several boats to capture the raiders.

The water was numbing cold, but Cushing made for the shore opposite Plymouth. In the wild turmoil he heard the Rebels hauling his men aboard their dinghies and making them captive. Several feet away he saw the outline of a man's head. Then a great gurgling yell welled up from inside the man and he disappeared into the pitch blackness. A Confederate launch, hearing the dying shriek, headed in Cushing's direction. He swam faster. While battling the river's strong current he heard his name called. Not recognizing the voice as one of his own men, he kept going.

Suddenly Cushing heard a groan a few yards behind him. Turning he saw Acting Master's Mate John Woodman, too exhausted to swim farther. Cushing held Woodman afloat for 10 minutes until the mate struggled free and sank like a stone.

For the first time since the Rebels discovered him, a great surge of despair swept over Cushing. He was now convinced that death was near. He preferred to drown rather than fall captive. Too tired to consciously battle the choppy waters, discouraged by not knowing whether his torpedo destroyed or even damaged the ram, Cushing was about to resign himself to dying. But his arms instinctively continued to draw back water and his legs kicked, though feebly as a mechanical toy slowly running down.

Finally his feet touched mud. In a sudden spurt of excitement at reaching land, Cushing tried to stand up, but, completely exhausted, he could only sprawl half-in, half-out of the water. For hours Cushing lay in the swamp; with daybreak the sun soaked up his weariness and he felt strength creeping back into his body.

Looking up, Cushing saw he was not 40 yards from one of the the emplacements guarding Plymouth. A sentry was walking the parapet. With a start, Cushing realized he was lying helplessly in the open. He wondered why the sentinel had not seen him, then guessed that the slimy mud camouflaged him perfectly. When the guard's back was turned,

Cushing dashed across the open space toward a thicket of rushes, but he only got halfway when the guard turned. Cushing fell forward, burrowing his elbows and feet into the mud.

A few minutes later, four Rebel soldiers came along a path several feet away. They nearly stepped on his arm as they passed, oblivious to the filth-caked Yankee lying near their boots. After slithering through the swamps for five hours until his arms and legs were scraped raw, Cushing was discovered by a slave.

"Are you one of them Yankees?" asked the slave, looking at the young Lieutenant as if he had come from outer space.

Cushing asked about the *Albemarle.*

"Sink her?" snorted the slave, repeating Cushing's question. "She is dead gone sunk and they will hang you if they catch you. I heard one of them say there's a hole big enough in her hull to drive a wagon through."

Cushing wanted to whoop for joy. Flusser had been avenged. His spirits buoyed up by the news, Cushing continued to crawl through the swamps until he spotted an unguarded skiff in the river. Swimming out to it, Cushing cut it loose and hung on behind with only his face out of water. The current carried him out toward the Albemarle Sound.

The banks of the Roanoke teemed with Rebel pickets searching for him. He could only hope that from shore the skiff looked like a piece of flotsam probably blown off the *Albemarle.*

At nightfall, Cushing wearily climbed on top of the craft and, using the stars to guide him, paddled for 12 hours to where he thought the flotilla was anchored.

Two o'clock the next morning Cushing made out the

The top of the Albemarle protrudes above the surface of the Roanoke River, as jubilant Union officials hail Cushing's daring feat.

Valley City lying at anchor. He hailed her.

The *Valley City* lowered a boat and approached him warily. When some of the men recognized Cushing, they refused to believe their eyes.

"You're dead!" they gasped as if looking at a muddy ghost. "You've got to be, or you would have returned 24 hours ago!"

Word spread quickly through the flotilla that Cushing had finally destroyed the hated *Albemarle*. Rockets were fired in joy as the news was wired to Washington and President Lincoln.

Cushing was given a vote of thanks by Congress, promoted to Lieutenant Commander, and later shared in $79,954 prize money with his men, all of whom either escaped subsequently or were exchanged as prisoners of war. Only two of his raiders died, both by drowning.

With the end of the *Albemarle*, the recapture of Plymouth was assured. As for Cushing, legends continued to magnify about him in the closing days of the war. They grew even more in later years. Cushing's future seemed bright. But a week before Christmas, 1874, he died in a Washington, D.C., hospital for the insane.

The origin of the most haunting bugle call was almost lost to history. Here is the unusual story behind the saddest and sweetest bugle call ever written.

"Taps" —
How The Famous
Bugle Call Was Written

Perhaps the saddest yet sweetest brief passage of musical notes are the 28 bars of the plaintive bugle call known today as *Taps*, used in the military to mark flag-lowering at the end of the day, to mark "lights out and all to bed" at night and to mark the end of a life at a burial.

Many words have been written to the modern *Taps*, and the most familiar ones readily evoke the notes themselves:

> *Day is done, gone the sun*
>
> *From the hills, from the lake,*
>
> *From the skies.*
>
> *All is well, safely rest,*
>
> *God is nigh.*

What is the history of these few notes that are so full of sad sweetness?

Their origin has been preserved only because an unsatisfactory version, by writer Gustav Kobbe, appeared in the *Century Magazine* for August, 1898. It brought a prompt correction and amplification from a reader who knew what he was talking about.

Kobbe had explained in *Century* that the first few bars of *Taps* were from a French song written for Napoleon by David Buhl, the name of which translates into English as *Napoleon's Favorite Song*. The remaining bars of *Taps*, said

Kobbe, were from England and had been derived from an Italian cavalry trumpet call. Kobbe said he did not know who had put them together in *Taps*.

The editors of *Century* promptly got a letter from reader Oliver W. Norton, of Chicago. *Taps*, he said, was composed off the top of his head by an illustrious Union General in the Civil War. Daniel Adams Butterfield, early in July 1862, immediately after the Seven Days Battle, while bivouacked at Harrison's Landing, Berkeley Plantation, on the banks of the James River near Richmond, Va.

Norton said he ought to know. He was Butterfield's bugler and he was the first bugler ever to sound what was then the "new" *Taps*. If the editors didn't believe him, he suggested that they contact General Butterfield, who was then a prosperous and well-known businessman living near West Point, N.Y.

They did, and Butterfield answered that he recalled "the substantial truth of the statements made by Norton." He then went on at length to review as best he could, after 36 years, the sad events that had led to his composing *Taps*.

When the Civil War broke out, Butterfield — who was born in Utica, N.Y., in 1831 — had been eastern superintendent of the American Express Co. in New York City. He was a chunky man, with dark, penetrating eyes and a thick, handlebar mustache that made him look older than he was — and he was a Colonel in the 12th regiment of the New York National Guard when called to the colors and given a Brigade and one star on his shoulder.

By July, 1862, the Peninsular Campaign in Virginia had gone badly, McClellan having failed to take Richmond. Nearly 11,000 troops on both sides were killed during the week of the Seven Days Battle. Butterfield's Third Brigade was severely gored on June 27 at the Battle of Gaines' Mill,

Oliver W. Norton, the first bugler ever to play Taps, revealed the true account of how the haunting bugle call was composed by none other than the illustrious Union General Daniel Adams Butterfield.

during which 602 of his men were killed or wounded. Butterfield later got the Medal of Honor for his gallantry in rallying his troops at Gaines' Mill against overwhelming odds. After repulsing the Confederates, his brigade covered the withdrawal of McClellan's Army of the Potomac to Harrison's Landing. Butterfield arrived there himself on July 2, 1862, and the decimated Third Brigade rested, recovered from its wounds and received replacements.

Butterfield's state of mind amid the heat, humidity, intermittent rains, mud, mosquitoes, dysentery, typhoid and general wretchedness in camp was marked by a sense of sadness. He had lost many old friends, as well as many young men committed to his command, while he escaped with only a minor wound himself. It was under these conditions, just before the 4th of July, that he heard again, as he had for so many months, the then regulation bugle call known as *Extinguish Lights*. The older call was also *Taps*, for the name was much older than the particular bugle call used.

Extinguish Lights did not seem sad enough to Butterfield for the mood of that July. He explained to *Century's* editors that, "The call of [the old] *Taps* did not seem to be as smooth, melodious and musical as it should be." He decided to compose something less formal and more distinctive, like another bugle call he had put together for his own men.

Earlier, though he couldn't write a note of music, he had invented a call to serve the same purpose as the Navy cry of "Now hear this ..." It notified his men that a regulation bugle call for their ears only was about to be sounded.

His troops had already put their own words to that one: "Dan, Dan, Dan, Butterfield. Butterfield." The general noted, however, that his men "in some trying circumstances" sang, "Damn, Damn, Damn, Butterfield, Butterfield."

Union General Daniel Adams Butterfield. Although he never sought any credit for composing the most famous of all bugle calls, considering it but a minor incident in his outstanding military career, he recounted the details some 36 years after he had written Taps during the Civil War.

Now, to compose a new *Taps*, he formed a brief melody in his head and had an aide write it down in musical notation from his humming and whistling of it. He sent for Norton, his 22-year-old bugler — then a Private in the 83rd Pennsylvania Infantry Regiment.

Norton (who later became a Major) told what happened then.

"Showing me some notes on a staff, written in pencil on the back of an envelope, he [Butterfield] asked me to sound them on my bugle. I did this several times, playing the music as written. He changed it somewhat, lengthening some notes and shortening others, but retaining the melody as he first gave it to me. After getting it to his satisfaction, he directed me to sound that call for *Taps* thereafter, in place of the regulation call."

That night, Bugler Norton took his accustomed position in camp, stood at attention, and, pursing his lips, poured out the plaintive strains of the *Taps* we now know, loud and clear. "The music was beautiful on that still summer night, and was heard far beyond the limits our our brigade," Norton recalled.

"The next day I was visited by several buglers from neighboring brigades, asking for copies of the music, which I gladly furnished. I think no general order was issued from Army headquarters authorizing the substitution of this for the regulation call, but as each Brigade Commander exercised his own discretion in such minor matters, the call was gradually taken up all through the Army of the Potomac. I have been told that it was carried to the Western Armies by the 11th and 12th Corps, when they went to Chattanooga in the fall of 1863, and rapidly made its way through these armies."

Taps soon replaced rifle volleys at battlefield burials,

because the volleys were sometimes mistaken by Confederate pickets for an attack. Quickly sensing the universal appeal for the melody echoing across no-man's-land, the Confederate buglers copied *Taps*. One of them sounded it at the funeral of Stonewall Jackson, less than ten months after Butterfield composed it.

Ten years after the war, in 1874, the new *Taps* was officially adopted by the United States Army. Its sweet yet melancholy melody has sounded countless times in the more than 100 years since then.

Butterfield never stepped forward to claim any credit for composing *Taps* until queried by *Century Magazine* at Norton's behest in 1898. Nor did he seek attention for it thereafter, or tell any biographer about it.

Perhaps *Taps* seemed inconsequential to him, compared to his civilian career and to his over-all military record. And it was only one of many bugle calls he devised.

He rose to Major General, was in 43 battle actions, suffered two wounds, won the Medal of Honor, became a Division and then a Corps Commander and later served as Chief of Staff for General Joseph Hooker and then General George Meade. He was severely wounded at Gettysburg, recovered, but was finally given non-combat duty after being stricken with a debilitating fever in Georgia. That he was innovative in the military is beyond question. Biographies that do not mention his composing *Taps* do identify him as the inventor of distinctive patches to identify members of different Army corps.

Butterfield could play the bugle himself, though he could not read music. He believed that a commander should have a *personal* call, so that when many units were in the field together the men could recognize bugle orders to them in particular. That was the purpose of his "Damn, Damn,

Butterfield got the Medal of Honor for leading a charge that saved the day for McClellan's flank at Gaines' Mill. His losses may have inspired Taps' sad mood.

Damn, Butterfield." It meant: "The next call is just for you, in my brigade, nobody else." He required each of his subordinate commanders to have personal calls and he composed the regimental calls for his Colonels in the Third Brigade.

He had a personal call for every one of his major commands, and one for the whole 20th Corps of the Army of the Cumberland when he was Corps Commander.

As a Division Commander, he led two-thirds of his division in retreat, at night, from the Second Battle of Bull Run. To keep it together in the dark he repeatedly sounded his personal bugle call himself, to be constantly answered by each of his regiments. By this means, he told *Century Magazine*, the whole command moved along in the dark "without loss of a straggler."

His civilian career made him a prominent American from the 1870's through the 1890's. He was into railroading, shipping, banking, real estate and the civic life of the nation

— the sort of private citizen whom governments turn to to head special commissions. He built a railroad in Guatemala, advised the Russians on the Trans-Siberian Railroad and tried unsuccessfully to get the job of building it. He studied European postal systems for the U.S. government.

Yet *Taps* outlives the memory of both his civilian leadership and his military valor, and joins a select company of famous melodies to come out of the Civil War, including *The Battle Cry of Freedom, The Battle Hymn of the Republic, The Yellow Rose of Texas, When Johnny Comes Marching Home* and *Dixie.*

Three years after he confirmed Norton's statements he suffered a stroke and made his own funeral plans. He died in July 1901, and was buried at West Point. His monument is one of the most ornate at the Academy. It was hewn from a 25-ton block of marble. An inscription records the 43 battles in which Butterfield fought, but nowhere on it is *Taps* mentioned.

On July 17, 1901, members of his old 12th Regiment led his funeral procession. Three rifle volleys were answered by a 13-gun artillery salute. Then the bugler sounded *Taps.*

A postscript was written to his memory on July 4, 1969, during the 50th Anniversary year of The American Legion. As an anniversary gift to the State of Virginia, the Virginia American Legion built a monument to Taps on the old Butterfield brigade campsite at Harrison's Landing. The setting is rich in other history too, for the Harrisons of Harrison's Landing and Berkeley Plantation included both Benjamin Harrisons and William Henry Harrison — two of them Presidents of the United States and one a signer of the Declaration of Independence. Their old mansion is still open to the public, only a short distance from where *Taps* was first sounded.

Monument erected by the Virginia American Legion on the campsite where General Butterfield composed Taps.

Captain Jim Waddell was more than a pirate — he was a Rebel raider and his mission was to destroy all enemy property at any cost. Who could have guessed that his secret plot was to destroy the Union oil supply in the Arctic? (The oil the Union needed for the war effort was not petroleum, but whale oil!)

The Civil War
In The Arctic

The morning fog finally lifted from Ponape Island in the Carolinas. Captain Jim Waddell, skipper of the Confederate States Cruiser *Shenandoah* scooped up his telescope. Sweeping Lea Harbor for signs of Yankee merchantmen he counted four ships at anchor. Their tall masts, broad flat bows and square sterns unmistakably stamped them as New Bedford whalers.

The *Shenandoah* was sighted almost simultaneously from shore and Waddell was somewhat puzzled to see a launch coming out to meet him. When it pulled alongside Waddell learned that the islanders and whalers, too, mistook the Confederate cruiser for an expected Union coastal survey ship. None of them had the slightest suspicion a Rebel raider was within a thousand miles of Ponape, especially on that April 1, 1865, so late in the war.

Waddell saw no reason to correct their assumption and the *Shenandoah* was ushered into the harbor where it anchored in 15 fathoms near the four whalers, *Edmund Cary, Pearl, Hector* and the *Harvest*. The Yankees, completely oblivious to their imminent fate, saluted the new arrival by running up the Stars and Stripes and waited for the newcomer to show his colors.

The tall and chunky captain of the *Shenandoah* twisted the ends of his drooping moustache and decided this was as good a time as any to reveal his April Fool's joke. Waddell lowered two whaleboats and two cutters filled with heavily-armed crewmen.

As the boats chugged toward the whalers, Waddell ran up the Confederate flag. Few of the whalers had ever seen the Stars and Bars before, much less ever having seen a Confederate warship. Just in case the New Englanders still did not realize they were now prisoners of the Southern States, Waddell forcibly drove the point home by firing a blank cartridge from his starboard Whitworth.

The whalers accepted their plight, realizing the futility of matching their harpoon bomb guns against a broadside from the *Shenandoah* They transferred their personal gear to the Rebel cruiser while the *Shenandoah* helped itself to fresh provisions and badly needed equipment. Then they were driven hard aground on the island's shoals and as a peace gesture for violating Ponape's neutrality, Waddell offered King Ish-a-Paw and his savages the chance to take what they wanted before the torch was put to the hulks. For the first time, native huts had wood flooring, their canoes canvas sails and even the copper sheathing was stripped from the whalers' hulls to make arrowheads, shields and breastplates.

The enraged skippers of the blazing whalers stormed to Waddell's face that he was a pirate second only to Sir Henry Morgan. Waddell patiently attempted to explain the South had long since sadly discovered it could not hope to take its prizes into neutral ports for adjudication. The Confederacy therefore was obliged to destroy its prizes, for only in that way could it hit back at the North's supply line. Besides, said Waddell, he was only following Navy Secretary Gideon Welles' instructions: "Do the enemy's property the greatest possible injury in the shortest time."

That the *Shenandoah* would shortly fulfill its orders in a wholesale manner undreamed of by Secretary Welles was

Confederate States cruiser Shenandoah.

indicated by this first of a series of telling blows from which New England would never fully recover. Before he finished, Waddell would seize 38 Yankee ships, mostly Arctic whalers, destroy 34 of them and only ransom the others so they could carry his prisoners home. This arsonist of the high seas burned a path of destruction costing the Yankees $1,361,983 in charred flotsam scattered from the Land of the Midnight Sun to the coast of Africa. In the mind of this Rebel sea raider, moreover, was the seed for a plot to seize San Francisco.

Waddell was born on July 13, 1824, in Pittsboro, Chatham County, North Carolina. His otherwise undistinguished early career was marked chiefly by an impetuous duel fought during his sophomore year at Annapolis with Midshipman Archibald H. Waring. Waddell came out of it with a hip wound that caused him to limp for the rest of his days.

Waddell resigned his commission when the war started and, joining the Confederate Navy, was assigned to coastal shore batteries until a secret mission sent him through the Northern blockade to Paris and then across the Channel to Liverpool where he quietly contacted James D. Bulloch, the Confederacy's agent in England.

Bulloch was paving the way for Waddell's incredible cruise by pulling off one of the war's cleverest pieces of international intrigue. The wily agent located two Confederate sympathizers, Henry Lafore and Richard Wright, both Englishmen who through secret codes and clandestine meetings agreed to act as dummy purchasers of two vessels, the sleek *Sea King*, freshly returned to London from her maiden voyage to Bombay, and the *Laurel*, a packet steamer running between Liverpool and Queenstown.

The *Laurel* was promptly advertised by its new owner for a voyage to Matamoras, via Nassau and Havana. But passengers and shippers who sought to avail themselves of the *Laurel* were courteously informed the ship was already booked.

An assortment of crates innocently marked "Machinery" and "Glassware — Handle With Care," but containing guns, powder and Confederate gray uniforms, mysteriously arrived at the dock. So did a weird assortment of passengers, the nucleus of the *Shenandoah's* future crew. As they filed aboard the *Laurel*, cautiously refraining from recognizing each other, they were handed dummy receipts for the 32-pound one-way fare to Havana.

The *Laurel* reached Funchal first. To avoid suspicion while biding its time until the *Sea King* arrived, Waddell told port authorities the ship's passengers were Polish emigrants bound for the West Indies and preferred not to come ashore. The *Sea King* arrived on October 19, was formally sold by its British owners to the Confederates States Government and commissioned the *Shenandoah*.

Work of converting her into an armed cruiser began immediately. Waddell was as pleased with the *Shenandoah* as a boy with his first electric train, and indeed he should have been for a prettier ship never slipped down the Glasgow ways. The new Confederate cruiser was a 1,160-ton, three-masted sail and steam ship originally designed for troop transport service to India. Under good conditions she could sail 16 knots or steam 10, an ability which seemed advantageous to Waddell both for chasing Yankees and being chased by their warships. She was 220-feet-long from bowsprit to stern, had a 35-foot beam, iron masts, lower yards and carried royal studding sails.

Waddell noted the ship's engines were small and of 180 horsepower, but reminded himself she was intended chiefly for sailing. Under steam her stack would be raised from its normally telescoped position and her propeller lowered into the water. Although the bunkers held 185 tons of coal, Waddell knew he'd have to go easy on steam because refueling ports would be few and far between.

Waddell gambled upon his powers of persuasion in recruiting a crew from those who brought her to Funchal. He was only able to talk 23 of a normal complement of 110 crewmen into enlisting, and at that they jacked Waddell's wage offer to a new high for mercenaries. The rest of the crewmen were put aboard the *Laurel* and instructed to tell inquiring Nassau authorities the *Sea King* had been wrecked and that they had been rescued by the packet. The *Laurel* then set sail for eventual blockade running duty.

The *Shenandoah* pointed her bow for the Cape of Good Hope, the first leg of a cruise to the Pacific whaling grounds. Carpenters worked tirelessly to ready her for battle should she be intercepted. They cut portholes for two 32-pound Whitworths, four 8-pound shell guns and a pair of 12-pounders, mounted in broadsides of four.

Meanwhile, officers worked side-by-side with the undermanned crew in building a powder magazine, while Waddell studied the sea for telltale signs of Union warships. Even with guns mounted he was a sitting duck. His green crew and patched together cruiser would be no match for a heavily-armed warship.

When at last the *Laurel* reached Nassau, the *Sea King's* sailors became boisterously drunk and told about the high seas commissioning. The American consul cabled Washington. The Navy alerted its European and Pacific squadrons and specifically ordered the *Santee, Wachusett, Iroquois* and the *Wyoming* to track the *Shenandoah* down and to obliterate it.

The *Shenandoah* tasted its first prize on the afternoon of October 30 when it met a Yankee bark. The ship spurted through the waters like a startled jackrabbit when Waddell fired a warning shot just ahead of its bow. After a two-hour chase, Waddell managed to place a shot between the Yankee's fore and main mast and she conceded. The captive was the *Alina* of Searsport, Maine, on her maiden voyage and carrying a cargo of railroad iron for Buenos Aires.

Waddell decided not to burn the *Alina* for fear the smoke might attract Union warships and ordered his crewmen to punch the bark's bottom full of holes. Some 45 minutes after she was boarded, the *Alina* ended her brief career. She was joined on the ocean floor by six more Yankee merchantmen during the next two weeks.

Nearing Cape Town the *Shenandoah's* engineer discovered the ship's propeller shaft and bearing were defective, presenting Waddell with a tough decision. Should he get back to full sailing strength immediately by putting into Cape Town for repairs and face the prospect of a possible blockade by the Union Navy? Or should he play it safe and strike out for Melbourne where Northern warships would be less likely to look for him? Intuition told him to head for Melbourne. It was a wise decision. The *USS Iroquois*, touching at Tristan da Cunha, picked up prisoners set ashore by the *Shenandoah* and steamed immediately for Cape Town where it figured the Rebel raider would refuel.

Bad luck again at Melbourne. British red tape nearly prevented repairs and during the drawn out diplomatic hassle several crewmen deserted. Worse, the long delay enabled word of his presence in the South Pacific to reach the Yankee whaling fleet of 40 ships.

But Waddell's disappointment at having the floating butcher shops flee long before he could reach the South Pacific fishing grounds was partially offset when 42 stowaways were discovered. Having sneaked aboard at Melbourne, they earnestly swore they were loyal sons of the Confederacy and eager to serve its cause, a vow Waddell found difficult to swallow in view of the high wages he was paying. He lost no time, however, in enlisting them.

The *Shenandoah* was at last adequately manned and eager for action, but long days passed uneventfully. Abandoning all hope of catching any lagging whalers, Waddell left the South Pacific. Heading north he met the neutral Honolulu trading schooner, *P. Fiert*, on March 29th. Waddell saw no reason to further advertise his presence in the Pacific and identified himself as a British cruiser. The *Fiert's* skipper mentioned he had seen four whalers at Ponape. Waddell streaked for the Carolines.

The Captain had plenty of reason for rejoicing that night. He ordered extra measures of grog for all hands as the whalers burned. Not only were the four ships ripe plums but he enlisted seven badly needed crewmen from among the 130 prisoners left at Ponape to await a passing ship. What's more — and this alone was worth more than the whalers themselves—Waddell found heretofore secret charts aboard the whalers. A quick study of them showed they were veritable keys to the Bering Strait and Arctic whaling grounds for they pinpointed areas where previous expeditions had reaped harvests.

He logically assumed the whalers, frightened out of the South Pacific, would head for the northern fishing grounds. And during the next eight weeks Waddell was to become the best friend the sperm whale ever had.

While Waddell watched the four flaming whalers dis-

The Shenandoah *fires on one of the 29 whalers she destroyed in the Arctic in her endeavor to cut off the Union's supply of oil . . . whale oil.*

appear over the horizon, the *Shenandoah*, a veritable ghost ship, was being reported in both hemispheres. The *Iroquois*, at Java, cabled Washington it was optimistic of shortly coming to grips with the raider. The *Wachusett*, reporting from St. Pierre, Martinique, said it was stalking the quarry and should, within a day or two, have the honor to report its destruction. The *USS Suwanee*, anchored at Bahia, Brazil, enthusiastically told Washington it was tracking down a report the cruiser had been spotted nearby. But no federal warship ever made contact with the *Shenandoah*.

In 20 days the weather turned from tropical extremes to icy cold as the *Shenandoah* headed north. Days grew longer. The sun, when it poked through the misty fog, rose at 3:00 in the morning and set at 9:00. Dozens of whales were sighted daily but no whaling ships. Doublechecking his calculations Waddell grew increasingly worried over their ability to plow through ice floes which got bigger with every passing day.

The beginning of the end for the Yankee whaling fleet came on June 22, in 62 degrees North Latitude when chunks of whale meat, a positive sign of nearby whalers at work, floated past the Within an hour Waddell sighted two whalers. He hailed them with a significant shot. The captives were the *William Thompson*, the largest New Bedford whaler afloat and the *Euphrates*. Both were quickly burned and the *Shenandoah* steamed off in search of more prey as the blazing hulks drifted lazily among the icebergs.

More whalers were sighted the next day, one of them the *Milo*.

"What are you doing all the way up here?" asked its skipper, stunned at the sight of the Stars and Bars. "I thought we escaped you down in the South Pacific. Haven't you heard the war is over?"

Waddell was skeptical. He couldn't blame the skipper for concocting any lie to save his ship.

"But I heard in San Francisco last April that your General Lee surrendered at Appomattox," insisted the *Milo's* captain.

Waddell shrugged off the protests as waterfront scuttlebutt. he released the *Milo* under bond payable when the South won the war providing she returned to New England, taking with her the *Shenandoah's* prisoners, a source of worry to the security-conscious Waddell.

During the next four days the novelty of capturing and burning began to wear off. Sometimes they were caught and fired in groups of twos and sometimes threes. Waddell caught and burned four at one spectacular stroke. The decks became so clogged with prisoners that he ordered them into whaleboats when the weather was clear. The whaleboats, sometimes 24 of them at once, were strung out in the *Shenandoah's* wake like a kite tail.

Waddell was jolted momentarily when he boarded the *Susan Abigail* and learned from San Francisco newspapers aboard that Lee had surrendered, Richmond had been evacuated — all while Waddell was at Ponape. But he took heart from a story in the same papers. Jeff Davis proclaimed that the war would continue. This was good enough for Waddell and also for a considerable number of his Yankee prisoners who asked to sign up as crewmen.

Waddell hit the jackpot at 1:30 on the afternoon of June 27. His lookout triumphantly called out 11 sails in East Cape Bay, Bering Strait. Such a plum far exceeded any of Waddell's fondest hopes of heaping glory upon himself and the Confederacy. If he could pull it off the coup would be a Rebel sea triumph rivaling the land victory at Manassas.

Confederate President Jefferson Davis proclaimed the Civil War would continue, in spite of Lee's surrender, and the capture of Richmond. That was all Waddell needed to hear - he continued to send Union whalers to the bottom.

All 11 of the whalers were windward of the *Shenandoah* and Waddell was a clever enough strategist to realize that he could only hope to bag all of them if he waited for a calm. Waddell snapped orders to lower the *Shenandoah's* stack, to bank her fires and to luff sails.

Tension increased hourly as Waddell looked hungrily at the distant whalers. Thanks to this Land of the Midnight Sun, he had little fear of losing his quarry during the night. But the wind wasn't ready to yield the Yankees. Waddell came back up on deck after finding sleep impossible and restlessly paced the deck until 10:00 o'clock that morning when a calm finally set in.

Running up a captured American flag, the *Shenandoah* steamed into the midst of the 11 whalers who accepted him just as warmly as those at Ponape. Waddell felt hundreds of Yankee eyes peering across the ice floes at this stranger, no doubt a Union cruiser come to pay it respects.

A boat put out from one of the whalers and a petty officer asked if he could please borrow a carpenter to help patch up his ship's starboard bow that had been punched in 20 inches below the waterline in a collision with an iceberg. Waddell, just as affably, said he would attend to the whaler's needs shortly and the petty officer returned to his ship after thanking Waddell profusely.

Within minutes five boarding crews went over the sides of the As they made to take the five nearest whalers, Waddell hauled down the American flag, upped the Stars and Bars and ran out his eight guns.

All but one of the whaling skippers surrendered. The captain of the *Favorite* mustered his reluctant crew and prepared his harpoon gun for action. Menacing the would-be boarders with a cutlass, the skipper warned them not to set foot upon the *Favorite's* deck or face the unappetizing prospect of swallowing a harpoon with seven dozen yards of rope as a chaser.

Taken aback by this suicidal challenge to a heavily-armed cruiser, the boarders returned to the *Shenandoah* for orders. Waddell would not be bluffed and guessed, correctly, that the balky captain was drunk. As the *Shenandoah* glided closer to the *Favorite* its skipper gaped into the ominous muzzles of Waddell's guns.

"When you fire, men, let her have it in the hull just below the waterline!" ordered Waddell.

The prospect of being blown out the water by a ship that out-gunned him eight times over and the resulting frigid grave sobered the skipper into surrendering meekly. The remaining whalers were made captive in doublequick time after Waddell served notice his gunners were overdue for target practice.

When Waddell heard of the plight of one of his prizes, the *James Maury*, he silently thanked his luck that he could find a plausible excuse for saving her. The *Maury's* captain had died during the first leg of the voyage. Aboard were his widow and two children who refused to give up his body to the impersonal sea. Shunning the crew's generous offer to give up their potential purses and to turn back, the widow told them to preserve her husband's corpse in a cask of whiskey until they returned to New Bedford where he could be given a decent burial.

Waddell bonded the *James Maury* along with the *Nile* and loaded his 336 prisoners aboard them, less nine who chose to join the *Shenandoah*. Late that afternoon the torch was put to the entire remaining fleet. Hollow blasts, like distant artillery fire, shuddered one whaler and then another as flames reached gunpowder stores. The blazing hulks drifted pathetically, and as the masts slammed down upon the decks and spilled into the sea, fiery embers gushed up from the ships and showered nearby icebergs.

The nine whalers were still spouting flame as the *Shenandoah* sailed north in search of more game. But Waddell had seen the last of the whaling fleet and when ice crowded dangerously in upon the hull he reluctantly turned southward for warmer waters.

Emboldened by his phenomenal success, he began to plan the capture of San Francisco. Censorship being unknown, the captured San Francisco newspapers were virtual scorecards showing the names and locations of Federal warships. One of them, the *Saginaw*, guarded the Bay. Waddell was a personal pre-war friend of the ship's captain and he knew him to be easy-going and not too conscious of shipboard security measures, especially so far removed from the battlefront.

Waddell's plan was simplicity itself. The *Shenandoah* would dash into San Francisco early one morning and ram the *Saginaw*. Heavily-armed crewmen would swarm over the decks and grab control of the warship's hatches, thus making her captive before she could resist. By dawn the city would lie helplessly under the guns of the two ships.

To make sure the *Saginaw* was still at San Francisco, Waddell decided to stop an outbound vessel. On August 2nd he boarded the British bark *Barracouta*, 100 miles off Acapulco, Mexico, and 13 days out of San Francisco. Waddell, who had for so long relied upon surprise in badly mauling the North's commerce, got the surprise of his life. The war, the *Barracouta* told him had been over for four months!

The C.S.S. Shenandoah *as she appeared after Waddell's bizarre plan to capture San Francisco was aborted four months after the end of the Civil War. Waddell was the last Confederate to surrender.*

Waddell swallowed hard. Not only had his Arctic efforts been useless but most of his destruction had occurred when the war had long since ended. He was the last Rebel to surrender, and the final shot of the Civil War had been fired from the *Shenandoah's* decks on June 22.

Sorrow hung heavily over the *Shenandoah* as Waddell ordered her guns stowed below decks, her ports boarded up and the ship painted white to resemble an innocent merchantman. He then set sail for Liverpool, managing to elude additional cruisers sent out to intercept him. Waddell handed over the cruiser to the British on November 5, 1865, when the Rebel flag was lowered forever.

Index

INDEX

INDEX

107

INDEX

Acknowledgements

Quantrill — The Civil War's Wildest Killer

This story originally appeared in the April 1959 issue of *High Adventure*.

An Inside Look At the Monitor And The Merrimac

This story originally appeared in the March 1969 issue of *The American Legion Magazine*.

Lt. Cushing's Revenge

This story originally appeared in the January 1957 issue of *Man's World*.

"Taps" — How The Famous Bugle Call Was Written

This story originally appeared in the August 1974 issue of *The American Legion Magazine*.

The Civil War In The Arctic

This story originally appeared in the February 1957 issue of *For Men Only*.

About the Author

PAUL DITZEL

Paul Ditzel, a historian and avid Civil War buff, has 18 books and over 600 articles for magazines to his credit, including those published in the *Readers Digest*. His best-selling book, *Fire Engines, Firefighters*, was submitted for a Pulitzer Prize in American History.

He holds a Master of Science Degree from Northwestern University, where he graduated with highest scholastic honors.

His well-researched and superbly written books and articles have won numerous awards.

Other Books In This Series

- **Corydon — The Forgotten Battle Of The Civil War**
  By W. Fred Conway

  Only two "Official" Civil War battles were fought on northern soil — Gettysburg, and . . . Corydon. Includes the bizarre Ohio River crossing of 2,000 Rebels on captured steamboats.

- **The Most Incredible Prison Escape Of The Civil War**
  By W. Fred Conway

  "The Thunderbolt of the Confederacy," General John Hunt Morgan, tunneled under the 4-foot-thick granite wall of the Ohio Penitentiary in an incredible and thrilling escape.

- **The Ruthless Exploits Of Admiral John Winslow —**
  By Paul Ditzel

  His great-grandfather had captured Bluebeard The Pirate, but Winslow sent to the bottom another buccaneer whose depredations made Bluebeard's look trifling by comparison.

If not available at your favorite bookstore,
please order direct.